Becoming a High-Authority Digital Personality

Develop a Signature Style That Makes You Unforgettable

By Joe Correa

Published by Live Stronger Faster

This book is for educational and informational purposes only. The author and publisher are not engaged in rendering legal, financial, or other professional advice. Readers should consult a qualified professional before making any financial decisions.

First Edition

Table of Contents

Introduction

There is a pivotal moment in every creator's journey when technical skills, charisma, body language, storytelling, and delivery all converge into something bigger—something that shifts a creator from simply appearing on camera to *owning* the space. That moment is when you evolve from being "someone who makes videos" to being a *recognizable personality with authority, influence, and a signature presence.* Book 10 is the culmination of every lesson in this 10-book mastery system, guiding you through the transformation that turns creators into leaders, educators into icons, and everyday individuals into unforgettable digital personalities whose presence commands trust and attention before they even speak. This book isn't about tricks or superficial polish; it's about identity, resonance, intentionality, and the deeper psychology behind why certain creators rise above the noise while others blend into the background. It's about shaping the version of you that an audience can instantly recognize—through your voice, your style, your energy, your values, your delivery, and your on-camera ecosystem.

The digital world is overflowing with creators, but it is *not* overflowing with leaders. Most people show up on video uncertain of who they want to be, trying to mimic trending personalities, or diluting their unique strengths by chasing what already exists. High-authority creators do the opposite: they know exactly what they stand for, what they offer, what they don't waste time on, and what emotional landscape they create on camera. They have a defined style—not because they artificially created one, but because they learned how to refine and amplify what makes them distinctive. Audiences trust them because they feel grounded, intentional, and consistent. They deliver the same energy every time. They speak in rhythms that feel trustworthy. They create content that reflects depth, clarity, confidence, and a specific worldview. Their presence doesn't happen by accident. It's built, brick by brick, through self-awareness, deliberate practice, psychological mastery, personal branding, and the courage to show up as the strongest, clearest version of themselves.

High-authority digital personalities are not defined by loudness, perfection, or flawless performance. They are defined by *alignment*. Everything about them feels congruent—their tone matches their message, their visuals match their identity, their delivery matches their values, and their audience feels a sense of continuity whether they're watching a polished YouTube video, an unfiltered live stream, a short-form clip, or a podcast interview. This consistency is what allows them to scale trust quickly and deeply. When someone encounters them online, the first impression feels like the tenth. When they speak, people listen. When they teach, people believe them. When they lead, people follow. And when they disappear, people wait for their return. Authority isn't something you declare—it's something your audience senses. And this book is designed to help you build that sense intentionally and powerfully.

Developing a signature digital identity means learning how to bring together your natural strengths, your personal story, your communication style, and your professional goals into a presence that cannot be mistaken for anyone else. Your signature style is your creative fingerprint. It's found in the way you articulate ideas, the pacing of your delivery, the emotional energy you bring to a topic, the colors or lighting you're naturally drawn to, the types of phrases you repeat, and the way you carry yourself in moments of silence. It's also shaped by how you handle conflict, how you share personal truths, how you teach complex concepts, and how you navigate attention in a fast-moving digital world. When you cultivate this signature style, your content no longer competes in the algorithm—it becomes the kind of content your audience actively seeks out. You become memorable without trying. You become trustworthy without forcing it. You become a brand without needing to brand yourself artificially.

Authority also comes from how you frame your ideas. People follow creators who position themselves as thought leaders, even if their niche is small. They gravitate toward personalities who articulate insights clearly, who unify concepts rather than scatter them, who make complicated topics easy to understand, and who communicate with conviction—not aggression, not arrogance, but certainty. When you speak with clarity and purpose, you eliminate doubt in the viewer's mind. This is why Book 10 goes deeply into frameworks, language patterns, and psychological anchoring techniques that help you express ideas in ways that feel authoritative, modern, organized, and intellectually powerful. It also explores how to create emotional safety, how to command attention in quiet ways, and how to speak from a place of lived wisdom rather than borrowed confidence.

To become a high-authority digital personality, you must also decide what your on-camera identity stands *against*. Audiences resonate with creators who have boundaries—creators who don't shapeshift based on the trend of the week or soften their stance to avoid criticism. Authority is not about being an influencer; it's about being a leader who is unafraid to say, "This is what I believe, this is what I teach, and this is why it matters." It means having a mission that runs deeper than content, a message that transcends individual videos, and a direction that guides your creativity even during moments of uncertainty. This book will help you craft that mission with clarity, so your audience knows exactly what to expect from you and why following you benefits their lives.

Finally, becoming a high-authority personality means developing an inner state that matches the presence you want to project. Many creators try to build confidence from the outside in—perfecting lighting, wardrobe, gear, and scripts. But genuine authority is built from the inside out. It shows up in the stillness behind your eyes, the groundedness of your breathing, the intention behind your gestures, and the ease with which you occupy the digital space. It emerges from emotional mastery, self-trust, disciplined execution, and the ability to handle pressure, criticism, and visibility with grace. This book will guide you through building that internal foundation so that your presence is not just performed—it's embodied. The work you do here becomes the engine that powers your entire on-camera ecosystem.

By the end of this book, you will not only understand what makes digital personalities unforgettable—you will *be* one. You will have a clear signature identity, a defined on-camera presence, a consistent communication style, and an authoritative voice that commands attention without yelling for it. You will be able to step into any video format—short form, long form, live, scripted, or unscripted—and bring the same recognizable energy that your audience has learned to trust. Book 10 completes your transformation. From this point forward, you're not just producing content. You're leading a movement, building a legacy, and showing up in the digital world as the strongest, most memorable version of yourself.

Chapter 1

The Anatomy of an Unforgettable Digital Identity

A high-authority digital personality is not the result of luck, viral moments, or accidentally stumbling into relevance. It is a deliberately crafted identity built on psychological influence, internal clarity, consistent expression, and a deep understanding of how the human brain responds to presence. In today's creator landscape—where millions of voices compete for attention—the creators who rise above the noise are the ones who have a clear, recognizable, emotionally resonant identity that the audience can instantly associate with value and trust. Before you master technique, scripts, gear, or editing, you must understand the anatomy of a digital identity that sticks in people's minds long after your video ends. This chapter reveals how to build that foundation so everything you create feels aligned, recognizable, and distinctly yours.

Every unforgettable digital personality begins with **identity clarity**, the ability to define who you are on camera in a way that is specific, aligned, and strategically positioned. Most creators water down their presence because they keep trying to be everything: approachable but authoritative, funny but serious, raw but polished, niche but broad. When your identity is undefined, your audience doesn't know how to categorize you, and the human brain only builds trust with identities it can categorize quickly. Identity clarity means choosing what you want to project and what you will not. It means knowing your core message, your core tone, and your core emotional impact. It means having a mission so clear that people know, within seconds, what you stand for and what kind of transformation or value they can expect from you. Without identity clarity, no amount of camera skill will make you memorable.

Once you know who you are on camera, you need a **signature emotional resonance**, the emotional atmosphere you consistently bring into your videos. Audiences do not remember creators because of facts, instructions, or tactics—they remember how creators make them feel. Some creators make people feel energized, others make viewers feel grounded, some create a sense of safety, others spark ambition or curiosity. Emotional resonance is the invisible force shaping how your audience perceives you. If your emotional resonance is inconsistent, your authority weakens because people can't predict what version of you will show up. Authority grows when your emotional energy becomes predictable in the best way—whether you're speaking, teaching, storytelling, or debating. This chapter teaches you how to identify the emotional tone that aligns with your personality and niche, and how to intentionally maintain it across videos.

Another pillar of unforgettable digital identity is **communication congruence**—the alignment between your tone, delivery, visuals, and message. A creator discussing serious topics with a rushed delivery, chaotic background, and inconsistent energy creates cognitive dissonance for the viewer. The brain senses something is off. High-authority creators maintain congruence: their visuals match their values, their tone matches their message, their body language reinforces their words, and their delivery supports the emotional outcome they aim to produce. Congruence builds trust. Incongruence repels it. Your identity becomes stronger when every part of your on-camera expression is aligned, creating an immersive, predictable experience for viewers.

A high-authority digital personality also possesses a **signature communication framework**, a recognizable way of structuring thoughts, articulating insights, and simplifying complexity. Audiences follow clarity. People trust those who can organize ideas in ways that feel logical, digestible, and grounded. The greatest digital personalities—regardless of niche—develop their own rhythm of speaking, their own way of explaining ideas, their own conversational cadence. When your communication becomes distinctive, you no longer compete with other creators because your audience prefers your way of thinking over anyone else's. This chapter will help you develop the beginnings of your signature framework through repetition, articulation practice, and style refinement.

Your digital identity is also shaped by **intentional repetition**, the strategic reinforcement of phrases, concepts, values, and stylistic choices. Repetition is not redundancy; it's branding. The human brain trusts what feels familiar. When viewers repeatedly encounter your signature phrases, your consistent energy, your recognizable patterns, they begin forming emotional associations that strengthen your authority. You become the person they quote, the person they reference, the person they think of when certain topics arise. In crowded niches, repetition is what creates mental ownership. This chapter walks you through how to use repetition to build authority without becoming predictable in a boring way.

Another foundational element is **boundary-based positioning**, the ability to define not only who you are but also what you stand against. Viewers trust creators who draw lines. You cannot build authority if you appear afraid to take stances, avoid strong opinions, or constantly soften your perspective to avoid criticism. Boundaries make your identity firm. Boundaries make your presence sharper. Boundaries create polarity—and polarity is what forms loyal audiences. When a creator is too soft, too vague, too agreeable, too adaptive, their authority dissolves. Authority requires conviction, clarity, and the willingness to stand on firm ground even when viewers disagree. This chapter helps you articulate the boundaries that strengthen your digital identity and distinguish you from the thousands of creators repeating the same ideas.

A high-authority digital personality also emerges from **internal centeredness**, the emotional grounding that allows you to show up consistently strong regardless of pressure, views, criticism, or performance dips. Many creators crumble under negative comments, algorithm fluctuations, or moments of visible discomfort. Audiences sense that fragility, and authority weakens instantly. But when you display calm assertiveness, emotional control, and a grounded presence—even in live streams, debates, or emotionally charged content—your authority grows exponentially. The psychology behind this lies in mirror neurons: humans instinctively trust those who maintain composure. This chapter teaches internal grounding practices that increase your on-camera presence, mental clarity, and emotional strength.

Finally, the anatomy of a high-authority digital identity includes **visual distinction**, the subtle but powerful elements of your appearance, camera framing, color palette, backdrop, wardrobe, and lighting that create visual recognition. While this is not a branding book, the visual ecosystem surrounding you affects how viewers perceive your authority. Sloppy, inconsistent, or chaotic visuals undermine your message even if your communication is strong. Intentional visuals reinforce authority. When your visual signature is consistent, people start to recognize your content before hearing your voice. Visual distinction is not about perfection; it's about recognizability and cohesion. This chapter helps you understand the basics of visual consistency without requiring expensive equipment or professional studios.

By mastering these elements—identity clarity, emotional resonance, communication congruence, signature frameworks, intentional repetition, boundary positioning, internal centeredness, and visual distinction—you create a digital identity that feels unforgettable, trustworthy, grounded, and unmistakably yours. The greatest creators aren't just good on camera. They are consistent, recognizable, and psychologically resonant. After completing this chapter, you will begin shaping a presence that no one else can imitate, a personality that attracts loyal viewers, and a voice that carries weight across every platform. This is the foundation on which high-authority digital influence is built.

"The Creator Who Nobody Could Ignore"

Julian had been making videos for almost a year, but nobody seemed to remember him. He wasn't terrible on camera—he was polite, articulate, friendly, and well-intentioned—but none of that translated into presence. People would comment once and never return. Some videos would get a spike of views only to fade into silence within hours. Julian knew something was missing, something foundational, something deeper than editing or equipment. The moment he realized the truth was during a creator meetup when someone said they had "definitely seen his content before" but couldn't recall anything he said or what his channel was about. That comment stung more than any negative review. Julian didn't want to be forgettable. He wanted to be a creator whose presence lingered. A creator whose energy carried weight. A creator nobody could ignore.

One evening, reflecting on his stagnant channel, Julian began studying creators who had risen rapidly in the past year. Not the viral ones—but the ones whose audiences trusted them deeply. He noticed something he had overlooked: the creators who grew the fastest weren't necessarily the funniest, smartest, or most technically skilled. They were the most *defined.* They walked into every video with a clear sense of who they were. They had unmistakable energy. They didn't blend in—they carved out their own psychological territory. Julian started taking notes about their voices, gestures, pacing, emotional tone, and visual presence. He realized that while he had been obsessing over "what to say," these creators had mastered "how to exist on camera." Determined to transform, Julian began with identity clarity. He asked himself questions he had avoided before: Who am I when I'm at my best? What emotional impact do I want to leave? What am I unwilling to compromise? What do I want people to say behind my back? Slowly, answers emerged. He realized he wasn't the soft, overly accommodating personality he had been presenting. In real life, Julian spoke with conviction. He debated passionately. He loved simplifying complex ideas. But online, he had watered himself down, terrified of offending or being misunderstood. The result was a personality so neutral that the internet simply forgot him. That night, he made a promise to himself: he would stop diluting his presence.

The next videos Julian made were different—not because of new gear or new scripts, but because of new conviction. His emotional resonance changed. Instead of sounding unsure, he sounded firm. Instead of apologizing for his perspectives, he articulated them clearly. Instead of chasing trends, he expressed timeless ideas through his own lens. And something unusual happened: people started quoting him. They began commenting on how grounded he seemed, how steady his delivery felt, how refreshing it was to watch someone who actually believed in their message. For the first time, strangers messaged him saying, "Something about you feels different. I can't explain it, but I pay attention now." As Julian refined his communication style, he discovered his natural cadence—slow, thoughtful, measured, and confident. He began structuring his ideas with clarity, always anchoring each video around one core insight. He didn't rush. He didn't ramble. He didn't try to fill silence. Instead, he used pauses deliberately, realizing that stillness made his presence feel stronger. His visual environment became more intentional, too. He simplified his background, added warm lighting, and wore colors that matched his tone—deep blues, calm grays, grounded neutrals. He wanted people to *feel* something when they clicked on his videos: safety, certainty, clarity. Soon, viewers recognized his content without even seeing his name. His identity was becoming real.

The turning point came during a live stream. Someone challenged his perspective aggressively, expecting him to crumble or react emotionally. Instead, Julian remained calm, steady, and thoughtful. He acknowledged the viewpoint, explained his reasoning with clarity, and held his position with maturity. The chat exploded with admiration. People commented that they had never seen him so centered, so confident. That moment became a defining moment for his channel—not because of the argument, but because Julian demonstrated embodied authority. His internal state had caught up with his external presence, and his audience could feel it. Weeks later, at another creator meetup, something extraordinary happened. People recognized him instantly. They quoted his phrases. They referenced his frameworks. Some said they binge-watched his videos because "his voice made things make sense." Julian realized that becoming unforgettable had nothing to do with being louder or flashier. It had everything to do with being more *himself*—but the strongest, clearest, most intentional version of himself. The creator who had once been invisible was now a creator nobody could ignore. And his journey had only begun.

Chapter 2

Crafting Your Signature On-Camera Energy

Signature on-camera energy is one of the most powerful components of becoming a high-authority digital personality. Unlike charisma, which can fluctuate depending on mood or environment, signature energy is consistent, dependable, and intentionally designed. It is the baseline emotional frequency you bring into every piece of content, every live session, every short-form clip, and every audience interaction. Viewers rarely articulate it consciously, yet they feel it immediately. It is the reason some creators instantly command trust while others fade into the endless stream of content. Your energy is not simply “high” or “low”; it is a complex blend of emotional presence, pacing, tone, awareness, and internal state. The purpose of this chapter is to teach you how to intentionally design that energy so your audience perceives you as confident, grounded, and unmistakably distinct.

The first step in crafting your signature energy is understanding that all energy transmitted on camera begins internally. Many creators mistakenly believe that energy is something they produce outwardly through performance, hype, loudness, or forced enthusiasm. But true on-camera authority begins with **internal regulation**—your breath, your focus, your emotional clarity, and your psychological state before the camera ever turns on. If you enter a filming session frustrated, scattered, or anxious, the audience may not know the cause, but they will feel the tension. If you enter the session calm, centered, and grounded, your viewers will feel stability. Human beings are biologically wired to sense emotional signals instantly, even through screens. Therefore, before developing stylistic elements, you must strengthen your internal energetic baseline. This includes pre-filming rituals, breathing practices, micro-meditations, or simple grounding techniques that shift you into a clear and authoritative mental state.

Next, you must determine your **core energetic identity**, the recognizable energy that becomes your creative fingerprint. You must decide what emotional atmosphere you want to create every time you appear on camera. Some high-authority digital personalities operate with calm wisdom, others with focused intensity, others with warm encouragement, and others with bold certainty. There is no "correct" style—only the style that amplifies your strengths and reinforces your brand. The key is consistency. Unpredictable energy confuses audiences, while consistent energy becomes part of your identity. If your niche involves teaching, mentorship, transformation, finance, personal development, or leadership, grounded and confident energy builds trust. If your niche involves humor or entertainment, a playful energy builds connection. What matters is that your chosen energy aligns with who you are at your core, not with what you think the algorithm wants.

A crucial element of signature energy is **pacing**, the speed and rhythm of your delivery. Pacing communicates far more than words themselves. Fast pacing signals urgency, excitement, or anxiety. Slow pacing signals confidence, authority, or emotional depth. Most unforgettable digital personalities speak slightly slower than the average person, with deliberate emphasis and intentional pauses. These pauses create space for the audience to absorb information and signal that the creator is confident enough not to rush. Your pacing should reflect your message and your identity. A creator who speaks too quickly may seem nervous or uncertain. A creator who speaks too slowly without intention may seem unfocused. This chapter helps you identify your natural pacing and refine it so your delivery feels controlled, powerful, and anchored.

Another component of signature energy is **vocal tonality**, the sound and texture of your voice. Tonality shapes your authority as powerfully as your words. A tense voice makes you sound unsure. A monotone voice makes you sound unengaged. A wavering voice makes you sound apologetic. But a voice with resonance, warmth, or firmness signals authority even before your audience processes content. The key is not to imitate other creators but to develop your natural instrument. You do this through breath control, articulation practice, emotional grounding, and intentional use of vocal dynamics. When your voice matches your message, your energy becomes cohesive and magnetizing.

Facial expression also plays a major role in your energetic signature. Many creators unintentionally appear tense, distracted, or guarded on camera, even when their words are confident. This tension creates micro-expressions that the viewer interprets subconsciously as uncertainty. High-authority creators maintain relaxed facial muscles, intentional eye contact, and a grounded presence. Their expressions shift naturally—not theatrically. A calm face communicates stability, while a warm face communicates connection. Micro-expressions are subtle but powerful; mastering them allows your audience to feel emotionally safe and receptive.

One of the most underestimated components of signature energy is **stillness**. In a world where creators constantly jump, gesture wildly, and overload viewers with movement, stillness becomes a superpower. Stillness communicates confidence. A creator who can remain centered, grounded, and composed on camera appears in control. Movement is still important, but it should be intentional, not reactive. Over-gesturing dilutes authority. Under-gesturing can make you appear stiff. The right balance creates presence. Awareness of stillness also enhances your audience's perception of your message because it eliminates distraction.

Your signature energy is also shaped by **emotional intention**—what you want the viewer to feel by the end of the video. This intention directs your tone, pacing, posture, and eye contact. Do you want them to feel empowered? Understood? Challenged? Encouraged? Grounded? If you film without emotional intention, your energy dissipates. But if you film with a specific emotional outcome in mind, your energy organizes around that outcome, creating a more cohesive presence. Emotional intention is one of the most advanced forms of on-camera mastery because it requires a deep understanding of your impact. This chapter guides you through selecting emotional intentions that align with your brand and message.

Finally, crafting signature energy involves **repetition and refinement**. Your energy becomes stronger each time you express it intentionally. As you film more content, you'll learn what feels natural, what resonates with audiences, and what elevates your confidence. Over time, this energy becomes second nature—an unshakable part of your identity that viewers recognize instantly. This consistency is what transforms you from a creator into a high-authority digital personality. Your audience begins to trust not just your information but your presence. And presence is what endures long after trends fade.

When your signature on-camera energy is fully developed, your content becomes magnetic. Viewers feel drawn to you, even before they fully understand why. They listen more deeply, engage more frequently, and share your content more readily. They see you as someone with gravity—someone who delivers not just information but transformation. The work you do in this chapter will shape every video you make from this point forward, strengthening your authority, sharpening your identity, and helping you stand out in a digital world that rewards authenticity and psychological resonance. This is one of the most essential skills of your entire on-camera career.

"The Day Julian Found His True Energy"

Julian had been improving steadily—his delivery was clearer, his identity was becoming more defined, and viewers were beginning to recognize him. But something still bothered him: he couldn't figure out why some videos felt magnetic and others felt flat, even when the content was equally strong. The turning point came on a day when Julian recorded three videos in the same afternoon. The first one felt powerful, the second felt dull, and the third was so tense that he deleted it immediately. For hours, he replayed all three videos, studying every detail. Same room. Same lighting. Same script outline. Same equipment. So why did only one video feel alive? He replayed the first video again—and then he noticed it. His energy. Not the volume or enthusiasm, but the internal state behind his eyes. In the first video, he looked grounded and certain. In the other two, he looked scattered and rushed. That was the difference. Not gear. Not skill. Energy.

The discovery stunned him. He had assumed that energy was something he expressed outwardly—through hand movements, tone, or facial expressions. But what he saw on-camera wasn't performance-based energy; it was internal energy. In the first video, he had been calm and focused after a short meditation he'd done without thinking much about it. In the second, he had rushed into filming after checking stressful emails. In the third, he had recorded while frustrated with technical issues. Even though he hid those emotions outwardly, the camera had captured all of them. And the audience would feel them too. The camera wasn't just showing his actions; it was revealing his internal state. For the first time, Julian understood that his presence wasn't something he performed—it was something he broadcasted.

Determined to figure out his true signature energy, Julian filmed short clips experimenting with different emotional approaches. In one, he tried being overly enthusiastic; it felt fake. In another, he tried being overly serious; it felt stiff. In another, he tried being intense; it felt forced. Nothing clicked until he tried something radically simple: he centered himself. He breathed slowly. He grounded his feet. He looked into the lens with calm certainty and spoke from a place of intentional clarity. When he watched the playback, he froze. That was it. That was his energy. Calm. Confident. Direct. Grounded. It wasn't loud. It wasn't dramatic. It wasn't a performance. It was him at his best.

As he continued filming in the weeks that followed, Julian refined his pacing. He learned to slow down—not to drag, but to deliver ideas with intention. He allowed silence to exist between sentences instead of filling every moment with words. He noticed that when he paused deliberately, his messages carried more weight. When he spoke too quickly, he looked nervous. When he rushed for emotional impact, the impact diminished. But when he spoke with controlled pacing, viewers commented on how "clear," "steady," and "easy to follow" he had become. Slowing down didn't weaken his presence; it strengthened it.

Julian then turned his attention to his voice. He replayed his videos with his eyes closed, focusing only on the sound. In the early days of his channel, his voice had been tentative, almost apologetic. But in his newer videos, his voice had developed warmth and resonance. He could hear the difference. He wasn't trying to sound like anyone else—he was simply speaking from his diaphragm, grounding his breath, and allowing his natural tonality to appear. People began commenting on his voice specifically. They said it made them feel calm. They said it made complex ideas easier to understand. They said they trusted him more when he spoke slowly and clearly. Every comment confirmed the truth: his energy had become an asset.

One afternoon, Julian watched one of his earliest videos out of curiosity. It felt like watching a stranger—someone timid, someone disconnected, someone trying too hard. He realized just how far he had come. His old videos were filled with nervous movement, unnecessary gestures, and subtle facial tension. But in his new videos, he looked centered. He looked present. He looked like someone who believed what he was saying. And that confidence didn't come from success—it came from internal alignment.

The true test of his energy came during a collaboration with another creator. They filmed a discussion on creative confidence, and halfway through the session, the other creator started speaking rapidly, bouncing from idea to idea. In the past, Julian would have matched that energy out of discomfort. But now, he didn't budge. He stayed grounded. He spoke at his pace. He kept his intentional presence. When the video was published, the comments overwhelmingly mentioned Julian's energy. People said he seemed like the calm center of the conversation. People said they trusted his insights more. People said his presence gave the video structure—and authority.

That day, Julian realized something remarkable: he didn't just have a signature energy. He had a **stabilizing** energy—an energy that brought clarity to chaos, focus to noise, and calm confidence to any conversation. It was a type of presence people didn't just notice; they relied on. And for the first time, Julian understood that this energy wasn't just part of his digital identity—it was part of his leadership. He wasn't merely becoming a better creator; he was becoming a stronger, more grounded version of himself. And now that he knew how to cultivate that energy, he could build an entire on-camera legacy around it.

Chapter 3

Developing a Signature Communication Framework

One of the defining traits of a high-authority digital personality is the ability to communicate in a way that feels unmistakably unique. This is where your signature communication framework comes into play. It is not just the structure of your content; it is the rhythm, clarity, logic, and emotional flow through which you express ideas. When you develop your own framework, your audience learns to trust your way of thinking. They come to you not only for answers but for the specific style of insight that only you can deliver. You become a source of intellectual organization in a chaotic digital environment. This framework is one of the most powerful tools you can build because it makes your content easier to remember, easier to quote, easier to share, and easier to emotionally absorb.

A signature communication framework begins with **clarity of concept**. Every piece of communication must start with a single central idea. Viewers cannot follow multiple ideas at once, and trying to cover too many angles weakens authority. Strong communicators isolate the core message of a video before they begin speaking. They know the difference between what is essential and what is optional. Clarity is not about oversimplifying; it is about creating cognitive space for the audience to absorb the message. When you choose your central idea, everything else must orbit around it. The clearer your central message, the more powerful your delivery becomes. The brain trusts clarity. It associates clarity with intelligence. And when you communicate with clarity consistently, your authority grows naturally.

Once the central idea is defined, the next step is **structured logic**—your ability to present ideas in a sequence that feels intentional, easy to follow, and internally consistent. Structure creates a sense of reliability. Viewers feel safe when they know how your mind works. Some creators use a three-part structure, others use progressive steps, others use chronological reasoning, and others use contrast-based thinking. The specific structure you choose is less important than its consistency. When your audience recognizes your structure, they feel like they know you. Structure allows your ideas to land more deeply and creates an intuitive experience for the viewer. When your structure is recognizable, your content becomes more shareable because people can easily repeat the flow of your argument.

Another key element of a communication framework is **language precision**. High-authority digital personalities choose words carefully. They eliminate filler language, vague expressions, and unnecessary disclaimers. They speak with intention. Precise language does not mean sounding stiff or robotic; it means removing linguistic clutter that weakens your message. When your language becomes precise, your ideas sound more trustworthy, your voice sounds more certain, and your presence becomes sharper. Viewers subconsciously interpret precision as expertise, which strengthens your authority even if they cannot articulate why. One of the fastest ways to elevate your identity is to audit your language weekly and identify common patterns of weakness—rambling, repetitive words, apologetic phrasing, or over-explaining. Refine these patterns, and your authority multiplies.

Your communication framework is also shaped by **metaphorical thinking**. Humans learn more effectively through metaphors, analogies, and visual language than through raw information. When you develop your own style of metaphor, you become memorable. Some creators use scientific analogies, others use storytelling metaphors, others use emotional imagery. Whatever style you choose should align with your personality and niche. Metaphors create bridges between complex ideas and intuitive understanding. They give your communication a signature flavor. When you use metaphors consistently, your audience begins quoting you, referencing your analogies, and repeating your models. This is how your voice becomes part of their thinking process—one of the strongest outcomes of authority.

Another pillar of your framework is **rhythmic delivery**, the pacing and emphasis patterns that make your communication feel smooth, controlled, and compelling. Rhythm is the reason why some speakers captivate audiences even with simple content. Rhythm is not about musicality; it is about knowing when to speed up, when to slow down, when to pause, and when to emphasize. Pauses are especially powerful because they create space for emotional impact and allow your message to land. The more intentional your rhythm, the more influential your presence becomes. Over time, your unique rhythm becomes recognizable, giving your audience a consistent auditory experience that reinforces your identity.

Your framework also depends on **emotional anchoring**, the ability to attach your message to an emotional experience. People do not remember information; they remember how information made them feel. When you communicate with emotional anchoring—by triggering curiosity, clarity, relief, urgency, inspiration, or safety—your content becomes more impactful. Emotional anchoring must be intentional. Every main point should create a specific emotional moment. When your audience feels something at the right moment, the brain stores the message. This emotional precision makes your communication more persuasive and your authority more natural. To complete your communication framework, you must incorporate **conclusion mastery**, the ability to end your content in a way that feels complete, integrated, and purposeful. Weak conclusions leave viewers feeling unresolved, which lowers authority. Strong conclusions create cognitive closure. They reinforce the core message. They give the viewer a sense of completion. A well-crafted conclusion makes the entire message feel more cohesive, and the more cohesive your message feels, the more competent you appear. This final moment is your last chance to shape how viewers perceive you. High-authority personalities conclude with clarity, certainty, and intention.

When all these elements—clarity, structure, precision, metaphor, rhythm, emotional anchoring, and closure—combine, you create a communication framework that becomes as recognizable as your face or voice. This is what separates forgettable creators from unforgettable ones. When audiences feel the consistency of your mind, they trust your leadership. And when they trust your leadership, your digital identity becomes magnetic. Building this framework is not about sounding academic or formulaic. It is about developing a communication style that feels uniquely yours, elevates your presence, and makes your impact impossible to ignore.

"The Moment Julian Learned to Think Out Loud"

Julian's transformation was well underway, but he kept noticing one frustrating pattern: sometimes people understood him instantly, and other times they seemed confused even when he explained things carefully. He wondered why some creators could speak casually yet still sound smart, structured, and compelling. Meanwhile, he often felt like he was "talking in circles," trying to make a point but losing the audience midway. One night, while watching a creator he admired, Julian saw something he had never paid attention to before. It wasn't the creator's charisma or confidence—it was the way he **thought out loud**. His ideas weren't random; they moved in a clear sequence. Every sentence felt connected to the next. Every point had a beginning, middle, and end. His communication wasn't just natural—it was structured. And that structure made him feel like a leader.

The realization struck Julian hard. He had been so focused on presence that he had forgotten the importance of thinking clearly. His mind was full of ideas, but he wasn't organizing them before speaking. He'd hit record, start talking, and hope something coherent emerged. Sometimes it did. Often it didn't. He decided to fix that. The next morning, he sat at his desk with a notebook and wrote down a simple question: "What is the core idea of the video I'm about to make?" The question felt almost embarrassingly simple. But as soon as he answered it, a wave of clarity washed over him. Instead of rambling through five different points, he committed to one. That commitment made everything easier. When he recorded the video, it felt sharper. Cleaner. More intentional. When he watched it back, he realized he had just taken the first step toward developing his own communication framework.

Over the next few weeks, Julian experimented with different structures. In one video, he used three steps. In another, he used contrast—what people usually do versus what works better. In another, he used a small story followed by a clear insight. Each structure felt slightly different, but all of them gave his mind something to follow. His delivery improved instantly. He no longer paused awkwardly to search for the next idea because he already had the sequence in his mind. His viewers noticed too. Comments started rolling in: "The way you explain things makes so much sense," "I actually get it when you talk," "Your breakdowns are the best part of your channel." Julian felt proud. For the first time, people weren't just watching him—they were learning from him.

Language played a big part in his growth. Julian listened to his earlier videos and cringed at how often he used filler phrases like "kind of," "you know," "maybe," "sort of," and "basically." These phrases made him sound unsure even when he wasn't.

He started practicing speaking without them, choosing sharper, more intentional language. The change was subtle but powerful. His sentences became more direct. His ideas landed harder. His voice carried more weight. When he watched himself, he finally looked like someone who believed what he was saying. And when he believed himself, others did too.

One afternoon, something surprising happened. Julian was explaining a complex financial concept, and without planning it, he used a metaphor—comparing the process to water flowing through pipes. The moment he said it, the idea clicked in his own mind, and the explanation became clear. Viewers loved it. Dozens of comments mentioned how the metaphor helped everything make sense. Metaphors became one of Julian's favorite tools. He realized they weren't just communication devices—they were part of his creative identity. He began using analogies inspired by nature, engineering, psychology, and everyday life. Over time, viewers began quoting these analogies back to him. His voice wasn't just impacting people; it was becoming part of their own understanding.

Julian also mastered his rhythm. Early on, he spoke in long, unbroken paragraphs, racing through ideas without giving viewers time to absorb them. But as he developed his communication framework, he discovered the power of pauses. When he paused, something fascinating happened—the audience leaned in. Pauses made his ideas feel more intentional. They made his tone feel more authoritative. They allowed emotion to settle. He began using pauses the same way a musician uses silence—to shape the experience. This rhythm elevated his presence from informative to commanding.

The biggest breakthrough came during a collaboration with a friend, who said something that Julian never forgot: "You don't just explain things—you give them shape." That sentence stayed with him. It was the essence of his communication framework. He wasn't trying to sound smart. He was trying to make the world clearer. And that clarity was becoming his signature. Once he embraced that role, his confidence soared. His conclusions sharpened as well. Instead of trailing off or ending videos abruptly, he began closing with simple, powerful takeaways. These conclusions made his content feel complete, and viewers loved the sense of closure.

One evening, Julian watched a recent video and realized he finally sounded like the person he had always wanted to be—clear-thinking, grounded, articulate, and memorable. His communication had become a reflection of his identity. It was no longer accidental. It was intentional. It was his. For the first time, he understood the power of having a signature framework. It didn't just make him a better creator. It made him a more coherent thinker, a better teacher, and a more influential leader. And he knew this skill would shape every stage of his future—from digital influence to real-world impact.

Chapter 4

Building Magnetic Audience Trust Through Emotional Credibility

At the core of every high-authority digital personality is a deep sense of **emotional credibility**—the invisible quality that makes an audience feel safe, seen, and willing to follow your leadership. Emotional credibility is what turns viewers into loyal supporters, silent scrollers into subscribers, and skeptical strangers into trusting believers. It is not built through expertise alone. It is built through presence, emotional intelligence, and the ability to align your internal state with your external message. People are not persuaded by information; they are persuaded by the emotional experience of receiving that information. A creator with emotional credibility communicates in a way that feels grounded, stable, trustworthy, and consistently sincere. This chapter teaches you how to develop that emotional credibility and become the kind of personality viewers instinctively trust.

Emotional credibility begins with **authentic emotional consistency**, not performative authenticity. Many creators claim they are being "real," yet their tone, mood, and presence shift wildly from video to video. Unpredictability erodes trust, even if the content is strong. People trust creators who feel emotionally stable. When your audience senses that your internal world is grounded, they lean in. When they sense volatility, they pull away. This doesn't mean you need to be emotionally flat; it means your emotional expression should be intentional, congruent, and rooted in self-awareness. High-authority creators have a stable emotional core. They know what part of themselves they are bringing to camera each time, and they anchor their presence accordingly.

A powerful component of emotional credibility is **the ability to regulate your emotions in real time**. Viewers instantly feel when a creator is anxious, irritated, overly eager, or insecure. Even if you hide these emotions verbally, your micro-expressions, pacing, and tone reveal the truth. Regulating your emotions doesn't mean suppressing them—it means directing them. Before filming, emotionally credible creators take time to align their internal state with the message they want to convey. They release tension from their bodies, slow down their breath, and calm their nervous system. When they speak, their energy feels intentional and steady. The audience picks up on this emotional self-control and interprets it as strength, confidence, and maturity.

Another vital aspect of emotional credibility is **communicating from lived experience rather than theoretical distance**. Audiences can sense whether you are sharing wisdom you've embodied or simply repeating something you heard. Embodied insight has emotional weight. It carries nuance, texture, and subtlety that scripted or borrowed knowledge cannot replicate. When you speak from personal truth—whether it's professional experience, personal growth, or hard-earned lessons—your audience feels a deeper connection. This doesn't require oversharing or turning your content into therapy. It simply means speaking from your authentic vantage point. When you position your knowledge as lived, not borrowed, your audience begins trusting you at a psychological level.

Emotional credibility also requires **transparent confidence**, the kind of confidence that doesn't posture or pretend. Many creators adopt a "confidence performance"—a loud, exaggerated, or overly polished persona designed to appear authoritative. But audiences are extremely sensitive to emotional signals, and they can detect when confidence is forced. Forced confidence feels brittle. Authentic confidence feels calm, relaxed, and integrated. It emerges not from trying to appear expert, but from accepting your voice, your experience, and your worth. High-authority creators are not the ones shouting the loudest—they are the ones who speak with quiet conviction. This quiet conviction is magnetic because it feels real.

An often overlooked part of emotional credibility is **empathic communication**, the ability to understand what your audience might be feeling and address those emotions directly. Empathy is not softness; it is strategic emotional awareness. An emotionally credible creator acknowledges the fears, doubts, frustrations, and hopes that viewers bring with them. They speak in a way that makes people feel understood before being instructed. When people feel understood, they become receptive. When people feel misunderstood or talked down to, they resist. Empathy does not weaken authority—it strengthens it. It shows viewers that your leadership is grounded in respect, not ego.

Another essential skill is **emotional clarity**, the ability to articulate emotions as clearly as you articulate facts. Most people struggle to express their internal world, so when they encounter someone who communicates emotional truths clearly, they perceive that person as a stronger leader. Emotional clarity makes your content feel deeper. It transforms generic advice into meaningful guidance. When you can express emotions with precision, your message becomes multidimensional, and audiences form deeper emotional bonds with you. Emotional clarity is one of the fastest ways to elevate your digital identity from informational to transformational. A key component of emotional credibility is **emotional restraint**, the discipline to avoid reacting impulsively to comments, criticism, or emotionally charged topics. High-authority personalities do not take the bait. They do not display insecurity when challenged. They do not respond defensively or emotionally. Instead, they respond with perspective, composure, and intentionality. When viewers observe your emotional restraint, they interpret it as wisdom and strength. They trust people who can maintain composure under pressure. Emotional restraint also reinforces your identity—your audience learns that you are a stable, reliable presence, even when situations escalate.

Finally, emotional credibility is reinforced through **consistency over time**. Trust is not built in a single video. It is built through repeated emotional experiences that make viewers feel safe in your presence. When your emotional tone, internal steadiness, and empathic connection show up consistently across dozens of pieces of content, your audience begins to rely on you psychologically. You become part of their emotional environment. You become a voice they go to for clarity. You become someone they respect, not just someone they watch. Emotional credibility is the foundation on which long-term digital influence is built—and mastering it sets you apart from the overwhelming majority of creators who rely solely on technique or performance.

"The Day Julian Finally Became Someone People Trusted"

Julian had grown dramatically as a creator—his presence stronger, his communication clearer, his energy more grounded. But something still wasn't quite right. His audience liked him, but they didn't yet trust him deeply. They listened, but they didn't follow. They agreed, but they didn't commit. And Julian could feel the gap, even if he couldn't yet name it. The realization came unexpectedly during a live stream Q&A, when a viewer asked him a simple question about dealing with fear. Julian answered with helpful advice, but when he finished, a second viewer commented, "I feel like you're giving tips—but you're not actually *with* us." That comment hit Julian harder than any critique. He wasn't being accused of incompetence. He was being told he was emotionally distant.

That night, Julian replayed the live stream carefully. He saw something he had never noticed before: there was a subtle emotional barrier between him and his audience. He wasn't cold, but he wasn't open either. He spoke *to* them, not *with* them. His voice was calm, but not warm. His advice was solid, but not embodied. He looked confident, but not connected. It wasn't that he lacked skill—he lacked emotional credibility. He sounded like someone who had mastered the mechanics of communication without yet mastering the emotional depth that turned communication into connection. And as he watched himself, he realized something simple but profound: he had been speaking from his mind, not from his presence.

Determined to fix this, Julian began focusing on grounding himself emotionally before filming. Instead of diving straight into content, he spent a few minutes feeling his breath, noticing his emotions, and aligning himself with the message he was about to deliver. He recorded a test video after one of these grounding sessions, and the difference shocked him. His eyes looked softer yet clearer. His tone felt warmer without losing strength. His body relaxed naturally. He wasn't performing anything. He wasn't pushing confidence. He was simply *there*. When he watched the playback, he felt something he had never felt when watching himself before: he felt connected to the person on the screen.

Over the next few weeks, Julian began speaking from personal experience more often. Not in a dramatic or overly vulnerable way, but in a grounded, authentic way. Instead of saying, "Research shows fear is common," he would say, "I used to struggle with fear in ways I didn't even recognize." Instead of saying, "You should be confident," he said, "Confidence came slowly for me, and here's what helped." These weren't dramatic stories. They were simply real. When he spoke from lived experience, his voice carried emotional texture. His words felt warmer. His insights had weight. And the audience felt it instantly. Comments began appearing: "This felt real," "You seem more connected," "I trust what you say because it feels like you've been there."

But the biggest shift came when Julian learned emotional restraint. During a later live stream, a viewer tried provoking him with a critical comment about his appearance and delivery. Months earlier, Julian might have reacted defensively, subtly tense or dismissive. But now, something had changed. He felt grounded. He responded calmly, with clarity and composure, acknowledging the comment without letting it take him off balance. The chat exploded with admiration. People commented that his calm was inspiring, that his emotional poise made them trust him even more. Julian realized in that moment that emotional credibility wasn't just built through warmth—it was also built through strength.

A defining moment happened during a video where Julian talked about burnout. Instead of giving polished advice, he spoke about a time when he had pushed himself too hard, lost his clarity, and felt disconnected from his work. He didn't dramatize it. He didn't turn it into a confession. He simply told the truth in a grounded way. When the video went live, something extraordinary happened—people messaged him privately to thank him. They said it made them feel seen. They said it helped them acknowledge their own burnout. They said they didn't just learn something; they *felt* something. And Julian realized that emotional credibility wasn't about revealing everything—it was about revealing just enough truth to make the audience feel understood.

One evening, while reviewing older videos for comparison, Julian noticed how mechanical he used to sound. He had been confident but emotionally distant, articulate but unrelatable. Now, he saw a different version of himself on-screen—warmer, calmer, more present, more human. He realized that his audience no longer just respected his knowledge; they trusted his presence. And that trust was the foundation of something far bigger than view counts or engagement metrics. It was the beginning of him becoming a true digital leader.

Julian went to bed that night with a quiet sense of pride. He wasn't just improving his craft—he was growing as a person. He was becoming someone who could hold emotional space for others, someone who communicated from truth rather than technique, someone who audiences relied on not just for information but for stability. And for the first time in his creator journey, Julian felt like he had stepped into the kind of presence that could truly shape lives. He was no longer performing. He was leading.

Chapter 5

Designing a Signature Visual Identity That Enhances Authority

A high-authority digital personality is defined not only by voice, presence, and delivery, but by the **visual ecosystem** that surrounds them. Humans are visual creatures, and viewers often form their first impression of your authority long before you speak. This is why the top creators in every niche—finance, fitness, psychology, real estate, relationships, leadership, entertainment—develop a **signature visual identity** that feels unmistakably theirs. What most creators misunderstand is that visual identity is not about expensive equipment or cinematic aesthetics. It is about coherence, intentionality, recognizability, and emotional alignment. When your visuals reinforce your presence rather than distract from it, your content becomes more memorable, more trustworthy, and more psychologically resonant. This chapter teaches you how to design a visual identity that strengthens your authority and helps your viewers feel anchored in your digital world.

The foundation of a signature visual identity is **intentional consistency**. When your videos maintain a recognizable look, viewers begin to associate the visuals with your brand. This doesn't mean you must use the same background forever, but your visual choices should feel connected across your content library. Color palette, lighting style, camera framing, wardrobe tone, and set design work together to create cohesion. Inconsistency confuses the viewer's subconscious, weakening trust and recognition. Consistency creates cognitive ease, which the brain interprets as professionalism and reliability. When your visual identity is consistent, viewers know what emotional experience to expect before you say a word.

Another essential component is **emotional alignment**—your visuals should reflect the emotional environment you want to create. If your personality is calm and grounded, your set and wardrobe should support that energy through soft lighting, neutral tones, and minimal visual noise. If your energy is bold and motivational, your visuals may incorporate brighter lighting, more contrast, or stronger colors. Emotional alignment ensures your visuals and presence work together instead of competing. When your visual identity matches your emotional identity, viewers feel a sense of harmony that increases their trust and engagement. Misalignment—such as using harsh lighting while delivering gentle content, or loud colors while expressing thoughtful ideas—creates dissonance that weakens authority.

Camera framing also plays a critical role in how your authority is perceived. Framing communicates psychological power, clarity, and professionalism. High-authority creators rarely use awkward angles, overly wide shots, or distracting backgrounds. Instead, they frame themselves with intention. The camera should be positioned at eye level to create equality, or slightly above eye level to create openness and approachability. A shot that is too low creates unintended dominance or tension. A shot that is too wide makes the creator appear distant or small. Proper framing brings the viewer into an intimate, focused connection with the creator, making the communication feel more personal and engaging. When framing is intentional, authority becomes natural.

Lighting is one of the strongest psychological signals in your visual identity. Poor lighting makes even the most confident creator appear unpolished. Great lighting elevates your presence instantly. You do not need expensive gear—only intentionality. Soft, diffused light creates warmth and emotional safety. Strong, directional light creates contrast and power. Harsh overhead lighting creates unflattering shadows that weaken authority. Lighting that is too dim communicates low energy or emotional heaviness, even if the content is upbeat. By mastering simple lighting principles—diffusion, color temperature, and light placement—you can dramatically elevate the emotional impact of every video you produce. Another critical part of your visual identity is your **background environment**. Viewers unconsciously evaluate your space to assess your credibility. A cluttered, chaotic background suggests disorganization or lack of expertise. A sterile, empty background may feel impersonal or cold. But a thoughtfully curated background—a bookshelf, intentional artwork, subtle lighting accents, objects that align with your niche—can elevate your credibility instantly. Your background should feel like an extension of your identity. It should visually express the themes, values, and emotional energy of your message. Your environment speaks long before you do.

Wardrobe is another powerful signal of authority. You do not need expensive clothes. You need **intentional wardrobe consistency**—colors, styles, and tones that complement your personality and visual environment. Wardrobe that is too busy, patterned, or flashy distracts from your message. Wardrobe that is too casual may weaken your authority if it doesn't match your niche. Wardrobe that aligns with your emotional energy enhances your presence. Viewers subconsciously interpret your clothing as part of your identity. This is not about superficiality; it is about psychological coherence. When your wardrobe supports your message, viewers interpret your presence as stable, consistent, and trustworthy.

A signature visual identity also requires **minimal visual friction**—a visual experience free of unnecessary distractions.

Flickering lights, messy shelves, uneven color temperatures, shaky footage, or inconsistent angles disrupt the viewer's emotional connection. When your visuals are clean, stable, and polished, the viewer's attention stays on you and your message. Reducing visual friction is one of the simplest yet most powerful ways to elevate your authority. Many creators spend months trying to improve their delivery, unaware that their visuals are undermining their impact. When your visual environment supports your presence instead of competing with it, your identity becomes magnetic.

Finally, your signature visual identity becomes powerful through **repetition and evolution**. Your visuals do not have to be perfect from the beginning. They must be intentional and consistent enough to become recognizable over time. As your authority grows, your identity will naturally refine. You will experiment, adjust, and evolve. But the emotional core of your visual identity should remain stable. Over time, viewers should be able to recognize your content within the first few seconds. That is the moment when visual identity transcends aesthetics and becomes influence. The visuals no longer just support your brand—they become part of it.

When you design a visual identity that aligns with your message, your energy, and your authority, you create a digital presence that is psychologically powerful. Viewers feel like they know you. They feel comfortable in your space. They feel grounded in your presence. Visual identity is not about impressing the audience—it is about supporting the emotional environment you want them to experience. When done correctly, your visuals amplify your authority and help you become a creator who is not only watched but remembered.

"The Night Julian Realized His Background Was Speaking Louder Than He Was"

Julian had been feeling more confident than ever—his voice had strengthened, his communication had sharpened, and his audience was responding. But one evening, while scrolling through his comments, he noticed an unexpected pattern. Several viewers mentioned the same thing: "Your content is great, but your background is distracting." At first, Julian dismissed the comments. He thought people were being overly critical. But the comments kept coming. One viewer wrote, "I keep losing focus because your shelves look chaotic." Another said, "Your lighting makes you look tired even when your message is strong." The comments weren't mean, but they stung. He had worked so hard on his delivery—yet something outside of him was undermining his presence.

Curious and slightly embarrassed, Julian rewatched his last few videos, but this time he tried to see them as a stranger would. He noticed things he had never noticed before. His bookshelf looked cluttered with random items he had never intended to display: an old coffee mug, a stack of mismatched notebooks, a camera box he hadn't bothered to move. His lighting was inconsistent—some videos were too warm, others too cold. His camera angle shifted from video to video. Sometimes he looked powerful and composed. Other times he looked small and distant. It became painfully clear: his background was loud, chaotic, and emotionally disconnected from the grounded version of himself he had worked so hard to develop.

That night, Julian made a decision. He would rebuild his visual identity from scratch—not by buying expensive gear, but by bringing intention into every element. He began by clearing his entire filming space. Every object had to earn its place. He removed anything that felt cluttered or chaotic. He wiped down his shelves, took down distracting artwork, and rearranged the room to create a sense of calm and openness. Then he brought in a few intentional pieces: a warm lamp with a soft glow, a plant that added life without overwhelming the scene, and a few books that reflected his niche and values. When he stepped back, the space felt completely different—lighter, cleaner, more focused. It felt like a space where a grounded, confident creator lived.

Next, he studied his lighting. He noticed that harsh overhead lights made his eyes look shadowed and his skin look dull. He experimented with soft lamps, window light, diffusers, and reflectors until he found a combination that made his presence look warm and approachable. He wasn't aiming for cinematic perfection—he wanted emotional alignment. When he turned on his new setup, he felt an unexpected surge of confidence. For the first time, he saw a visual identity that matched the emotional energy he had been cultivating internally.

Camera framing came next. He realized that his previous videos had inconsistent shots—sometimes too wide, sometimes too close, sometimes slightly crooked. These subtle inconsistencies weakened his authority without him realizing it. He adjusted his tripod, fine-tuned the distance, and raised the camera slightly above eye level. When he looked into the lens, he felt different. He looked more open, more confident, more established. It wasn't dramatic—but it was powerful.

His wardrobe was the final piece. Julian had never thought much about clothing beyond comfort. But now that his visuals were intentional, his wardrobe suddenly mattered. He noticed that patterned shirts pulled attention away from his eyes and bold colors clashed with his background. He began selecting clothing that supported his emotional presence—solid, calming colors like deep blue, soft gray, and earth tones. When he recorded a test clip with his new wardrobe and setup, he was stunned. Everything looked cohesive. Everything felt aligned. For the first time in his creator journey, the outside matched the inside.

Julian uploaded the first video with his new visual identity. Within hours, the comments came in: "Your video looks great!" "This feels so clean and professional." "Your presence feels stronger than ever." But the most meaningful comment was simple: "I feel like I know you better now." That was when Julian understood what visual identity was really about. It wasn't about looking fancy. It was about creating emotional clarity. His viewers could finally feel the grounded, thoughtful version of him because his environment no longer contradicted his presence.

Weeks later, Julian compared his old videos to his new ones. The difference was astonishing. In the old videos, he looked like a creator who was trying. In the new videos, he looked like a creator who belonged. His authority wasn't louder—it was clearer. His presence wasn't bigger—it was more focused. He realized that becoming a high-authority digital personality wasn't only about speaking well or showing confidence. It was about designing a world—visually and emotionally—in which his identity could thrive. His background wasn't just a background. It was part of his leadership.

Chapter 6

Mastering Presence Through Movement, Stillness & Spatial Awareness

One of the most overlooked components of becoming a high-authority digital personality is learning how to command space—both the physical space around you and the energetic space within you. Most creators focus on words and visuals but forget that the human brain interprets presence through movement, stillness, posture, spatial alignment, and the invisible emotional signals that these elements communicate. Presence is not just about what you say or how you say it; it is about *how you exist in the frame.* Mastering presence requires understanding the subtle language of movement, the psychological impact of stillness, and the way your body communicates authority, confidence, or uncertainty. Your audience feels your presence before they process your message, and in this chapter, you will learn how to harness that power.

Presence begins with **spatial awareness**, the understanding of how your body occupies the visual frame. When you appear too small within the frame, viewers subconsciously perceive reduced authority or reduced energy. When you appear too close, they may feel overwhelmed or invaded. Proper spatial awareness means framing yourself in a way that shows enough of your body to allow natural expression without losing intimacy. This typically means keeping your torso visible rather than only your face, which allows your body language to support your communication. Spatial awareness also involves ensuring your posture is upright, grounded, and open. A collapsed posture weakens your presence, while an overly stiff posture communicates tension. You must find the balance between structure and ease, creating a presence that is confident, grounded, and fluid.

Movement is a powerful communicator, but only when used intentionally. Most creators either over-gesture to the point of distraction or barely move at all. Excessive movement makes your energy feel chaotic and unfocused. Insufficient movement makes you appear rigid or emotionally disconnected. High-authority personalities use **intentional movement**—subtle, deliberate gestures that support the message rather than distract from it. A single nod, a forward lean, a measured hand gesture, or a controlled shift in posture can amplify your authority more effectively than wild expressive motions. Movement should emerge naturally from your emotional intention, not from nervous energy. When movement is intentional, it communicates emotional clarity.

When movement is reactive, it communicates insecurity. Stillness is equally, if not more, important. Most new creators fear stillness because they mistake it for stiffness. But true stillness is the foundation of presence. It communicates groundedness, emotional stability, and confidence. When you are still, your audience senses control, focus, and clarity. Stillness gives your message space. Stillness allows your facial expressions and voice to carry emotional depth. Stillness helps your viewers feel safe in your presence. High-authority creators understand that stillness is not the absence of movement; it is the mastery of unnecessary movement. Stillness is composed. Stillness is powerful. Stillness is magnetic because it communicates a centered internal world.

To master presence, you must also understand **directional energy**, the invisible flow of intention that moves outward from your body toward your audience. You can "direct energy" with your eyes, your voice, your posture, and even your breath. When your energy flows outward, your presence engages. When your energy collapses inward, your presence weakens. Directional energy is not intensity; it is intention. You can speak gently yet project strong energy if your attention and intention are focused. Many creators unconsciously withdraw their energy due to self-doubt or distraction. This makes their presence feel passive, even when their words are strong. Directing your energy outward—toward the lens, toward the idea, toward the viewer—creates connection and authority. Eye contact is one of the strongest tools of presence, but only when used intentionally. Staring into the lens without emotional engagement feels robotic. Avoiding the lens too often feels untrustworthy. Mastering eye contact means learning when to look directly at the lens to connect with the viewer, when to momentarily look away to think, and how to return to the lens with intention. Your eyes communicate emotional truth. If your eyes are tense, darting, or unfocused, viewers feel your internal disconnection. When your gaze is steady, warm, and congruent with your message, viewers feel your presence deeply. Practicing calm, grounded eye contact is one of the fastest ways to elevate your authority on camera.

Breath is another powerful but underestimated component of presence. Breath regulates your emotional state, controls your pacing, and influences the tone of your voice. When your breath is shallow, you appear anxious or uncertain. When your breath is grounded, your presence becomes powerful and controlled. Before filming, take slow breaths that expand the belly and relax the chest. During filming, allow your breath to support your pacing. Pauses for breath create rhythm, and rhythm creates authority. Breath is the invisible force that allows your presence to remain steady even when discussing complex or emotional topics.

Posture also communicates volumes. A slightly lifted chest, relaxed shoulders, energized spine, and open stance can instantly elevate your presence. Viewers subconsciously read posture as a reflection of inner strength or inner doubt. A small shift in posture can transform how you appear emotionally and psychologically. High-authority creators continually maintain posture awareness without becoming rigid or robotic. Posture is not about posing; it is about inhabiting your body in a grounded and confident way. When your body aligns with your inner state, your presence becomes undeniable.

The final component of presence is **energetic congruence**—the alignment between your inner emotional reality and your external expression. If you try to project confidence without feeling grounded, your audience will sense the incongruence. If you speak passionately while your body expresses fear, viewers will feel something is off. Congruence does not mean perfection. It means authenticity. It means owning the emotional truth of the moment while directing your energy with intention. When your emotions, movements, stillness, posture, breath, and gaze all align with your message, your presence becomes magnetic. Viewers cannot articulate why they trust you—but they do.

Mastering presence through movement, stillness, and spatial awareness elevates your digital identity more quickly than almost any other skill. It transforms you from someone who simply appears on camera into someone who *occupies* the frame with authority. When your presence becomes grounded, intentional, and energetically congruent, your viewers not only hear your message—they feel your leadership.

"The Moment Julian Realized He Was Moving Too Much to Be Seen"

Julian had come a long way—his voice was grounded, his visuals intentional, his communication sharp. But something strange was happening. Every time he watched his videos, he felt like he was... distracting himself. His words were strong, but his presence felt scattered. He couldn't figure out why until one evening, while reviewing a recording, he saw the problem clearly for the first time. He was fidgeting. Constantly. His hands moved excessively. His shoulders shifted every few seconds. His head bobbed slightly with each sentence. Even his breathing seemed rushed and shallow. He stared at the screen and whispered, "Why am I moving so much?"

He hadn't noticed it before because he had been focused on everything else: scripts, tone, visuals, emotions. But now that his awareness had expanded, his unnecessary movement became painfully obvious. His gestures didn't match his message—they were random, anxious, and reactive. And suddenly it made sense why some viewers said his content felt "busy" or "unsettled." It wasn't the content. It was him. His body was communicating insecurity even when his voice communicated confidence. The realization was uncomfortable, but it was also liberating. He finally understood what had been diluting his presence.

The next day, Julian experimented. He recorded a video sitting perfectly still—so still it felt unnatural and awkward. When he played it back, he cringed. He looked stiff, tense, and unnatural. That wasn't the answer. So he tried the opposite—exaggerating his gestures deliberately. The result was worse. He looked theatrical, almost cartoonish. Neither extreme felt authentic. It wasn't about freezing or performing; it was about intention. He needed to find the middle ground between lifeless stillness and chaotic movement.

That evening, Julian sat in front of his camera, closed his eyes, and simply breathed. Deep, slow, intentional breaths. For the first time, he focused not on performing but on *existing* in the frame. When he opened his eyes, he felt different—more centered, more grounded, more connected to himself. He hit record, not to film a final video but to observe himself. He spoke slowly. He didn't force his hands to move; he let them move only when the message naturally called for it. He sat tall, but not stiff. He relaxed his shoulders. He let his breath guide his pacing. When he watched the playback, he realized he was witnessing a new version of himself. He wasn't performing. He wasn't hiding. He was present. Over the following weeks, Julian practiced presence as a skill, not an accident. He learned how to sit in stillness without feeling frozen. He discovered that a subtle lean forward made his message feel intimate and engaged. He realized that widening his chest slightly made him look more open and confident. He practiced bringing his gaze to the lens with intention rather than staring blankly. Each small adjustment changed how he felt and how he appeared. His presence grew stronger—not because he did more, but because he did less with greater purpose.

One day, during a recording session for a collaboration, Julian noticed something remarkable. The other creator dominated the conversation with fast gestures and jittery movements. In the past, Julian would have unconsciously matched that energy. But now, he remained grounded. He stayed still unless movement was necessary. He maintained eye contact with calm intention. And slowly, something fascinating happened—the other creator began mirroring Julian's stillness. The entire tone of the conversation shifted. The energy slowed, settled, and deepened. Julian had anchored the room without saying a word.

That moment stunned him. It was the first time he truly understood the power of presence. Not as performance. Not as posture. But as grounded, intentional, controlled existence. He had always thought influence came from speaking well or thinking clearly. But now he understood something deeper: influence also comes from how you *hold yourself*. How you breathe. How you occupy the frame. How you direct your energy outward. Presence wasn't something he learned; it was something he grew into.

Weeks later, after publishing a new video, Julian received a comment that made him pause. It said, "I don't know what changed, but your presence feels... calm and powerful. I listen differently now." He read the comment three times. This was the exact transformation he had been working toward. His audience didn't see the hours of breathwork, posture practice, and awareness training. They didn't see the awkward early attempts or the many recordings he deleted. They didn't know he had rebuilding his presence from the inside out. They only felt the result.

Julian leaned back in his chair and smiled. This was the kind of presence he had admired in others but never believed he could achieve. He now understood that presence wasn't about being perfect—it was about being intentional. It was about anchoring himself so deeply that his audience felt grounded through him. And as he continued to refine his presence, he realized that he was not just becoming a better creator. He was becoming a more centered, stronger version of himself in every part of his life.

Chapter 7

Developing an Irresistible Signature Voice & Vocal Authority

Your voice is one of the most defining components of your digital identity. Long before viewers analyze your message, they subconsciously evaluate your tone, rhythm, resonance, pacing, and emotional warmth. A signature voice does not mean having a naturally deep or melodic voice; it means developing a vocal presence that feels undeniably *you*, a sound that communicates confidence, clarity, intention, and emotional intelligence. In the world of digital communication, your voice becomes your instrument—one that either strengthens your authority or weakens it. Mastering your vocal identity is not about sounding theatrical or overly polished. It is about refining the way you breathe, articulate, and express ideas so that your voice aligns with your inner confidence and enhances your presence.

The first step in developing vocal authority is understanding that your voice is shaped by your **breath patterns**. Shallow breathing produces weak, rushed, or strained vocal tone that signals anxiety or insecurity. Deep, grounded breathing supports resonance and clarity. Breath is the engine of vocal authority. When you breathe deeply from the diaphragm, your voice gains richness and stability. When you breathe shallowly from the chest, your voice loses strength and emotional grounding. Before filming, take several slow, deep breaths to calm your nervous system and activate your diaphragm. A grounded breath creates a grounded voice, and a grounded voice creates grounded authority.

Another component is **vocal resonance**, the quality that makes your voice sound full and confident. Resonance is created by relaxing the throat, opening the chest, and allowing sound vibrations to move through your body rather than pushing your voice outward. Resonant voices are not necessarily loud—yet they carry weight. They feel warm, present, and emotionally connected. When your resonance is strong, viewers feel as though your voice fills the space around them. Weak resonance communicates hesitation or emotional disconnection. Resonance can be trained through breathwork, vocal relaxation, humming exercises, and intentional vocal warm-ups. When your voice resonates from a grounded internal state, your presence becomes magnetic.

Pacing is another essential aspect of vocal authority. Fast pacing communicates urgency, excitement, or nervousness. Slow pacing communicates confidence, clarity, and emotional control. The most authoritative on-camera voices strike a balance between fluid pacing and intentional pauses. Pauses are not empty space—they are moments of emotional impact. They signal that you are thinking, not scrambling. They allow viewers to absorb your message. They also communicate self-trust. Rushed speakers sound like they are chasing their own thoughts. Grounded speakers sound like they are guiding the conversation. By slowing your pacing slightly and using deliberate pauses, you create authority without force.

Vocal tonality—the emotional texture of your voice—is a powerful signal of your internal state. Tonality that is tense, sharp, or overly serious may create unintended emotional tension for your audience. Tonality that is overly soft or airy may weaken your perceived authority. The most effective tone is one that aligns with your emotional intention. If your goal is to empower, your tone should feel strong and encouraging. If your goal is to comfort, your tone should feel warm and grounding. If your goal is to challenge, your tone should be firm but not harsh. Tonality is emotional. Your audience feels your tone more deeply than your words. When your tonality matches your message, your voice becomes emotionally persuasive.

Another element of vocal identity is **articulation**, the clarity with which you form and express words. Mumbled, rushed, or unclear articulation weakens your authority even if your ideas are strong. Clear articulation communicates precision, intelligence, and intentionality. It does not mean exaggerating your pronunciation or speaking unnaturally. It means respecting your message enough to deliver it clearly. Articulation improves when you slow down, open your jaw slightly, relax your tongue, and allow each word to fully form. Over time, this creates a vocal presence that feels crisp and grounded.

Vocal authority also depends on **emotional congruence**—your voice must match the internal emotional experience you want to transmit. If your voice betrays anxiety, frustration, or uncertainty, viewers will sense the disconnect immediately. Emotional congruence does not require emotional perfection. It requires emotional honesty combined with intentional delivery. When your internal emotional state aligns with your vocal tone, your voice carries authenticity. When they misalign, your presence weakens. The most influential creators speak from an emotionally grounded place, allowing their voice to reflect truth rather than insecurity.

Your vocal identity is also influenced by **your relationship to silence**. Many creators fear silence because they believe it makes them appear awkward or unprepared. But silence, when used intentionally, becomes one of the most powerful tools of authority. Silence creates anticipation. Silence signals thoughtfulness. Silence gives weight to your message. When you are comfortable pausing before making an important point, your audience feels the significance. Silence is not emptiness—it is presence. When you master silence, your authority expands.

Finally, developing a signature voice requires repeated practice, experimentation, and refinement. Your voice will evolve as your confidence grows. You will discover new tones that feel natural, new rhythms that feel intuitive, and new emotional textures that reflect your personal growth. The goal is not to create a perfect voice; the goal is to create an *authentic* voice that consistently communicates strength, clarity, and emotional presence. Over time, your audience will not only recognize your voice—they will rely on it. Your voice will become a source of stability and guidance. That is the true power of vocal identity: it transforms your presence from informational to influential.

"The Day Julian Discovered His Real Voice"

Julian had been receiving more engagement, more meaningful comments, and more loyal followers—but something still puzzled him. A recurring comment kept appearing under his videos: "Your ideas are great, but sometimes your voice sounds uncertain." At first, he brushed it off, thinking people were overanalyzing. But one night, he recorded a video late in the evening, exhausted from a long day. His voice was tight and slightly shaky. When he played the footage back, he winced. He didn't hear uncertainty in his words—he heard uncertainty in his *voice*. It was the first time he realized that his vocal presence didn't always match his internal confidence.

Over the next week, Julian began listening to his past recordings with new ears. He heard inconsistency everywhere. Sometimes his pacing was rushed. Sometimes his tone was too stiff. Sometimes his articulation blurred his strongest points. He sounded confident when he felt confident and uncertain when he felt tired, stressed, or unfocused. His vocal presence was unpredictable because his breath and emotions were unpredictable. He realized something crucial: if he wanted to be a high-authority digital personality, he needed to master his voice—not just his message.

One afternoon, Julian experimented with simple breathing exercises before recording. He sat in silence, placed his hands on his abdomen, and breathed deeply. When he spoke afterward, his voice sounded different—warmer, deeper, more grounded. He recorded a short clip without thinking much of it. But when he watched it back, he felt a jolt of recognition. This was the version of his voice he had always wanted: calm, assured, intentional. Not loud. Not forceful. Just steady. It was the voice of someone who believed what he was saying.

Intrigued, Julian began studying vocal techniques. He practiced humming to build resonance. He experimented with pacing, slowing himself down until his words felt heavy with meaning. He allowed himself to pause mid-sentence, trusting that the silence would hold. At first, it felt unnatural. But over time, it began to feel powerful. His pauses were no longer moments of hesitation—they were moments of presence. His tone no longer sounded pushed—it sounded authentic. He could feel himself growing into his voice.

The turning point came during a video where he spoke about the fear of starting. He approached the topic gently, allowing his breath to guide his tone. He paused often, letting the weight of his words settle. When he finished the recording, he felt like he had just spoken from a deeper place within himself. When he posted the video, the reaction stunned him. Comment after comment mentioned his voice: "There's something calming about the way you speak," "Your tone made me feel safe," "I finally understand this because of how you explained it." For the first time, viewers weren't just hearing him—they were *feeling* him.

Julian realized that his voice wasn't just sound. It was emotional communication. It was leadership. It was the bridge between his inner clarity and the audience's understanding. As he continued refining his voice, something profound happened. His presence began to shift even in his offline life. He spoke more clearly in conversations. He paused thoughtfully before responding. His breath became steadier. His tone became more intentional. He felt more grounded—not just on camera, but everywhere.

One evening, while filming a collaboration video, the other creator spoke rapidly and loudly, trying to impress the audience. In the past, Julian might have matched that energy to avoid seeming weak. But now, he stayed grounded. His voice remained calm, steady, and clear. After the session, several viewers commented that Julian's voice felt like "the anchor of the conversation." That comment meant more to him than any praise he had ever received. It meant that his presence wasn't just improving—his voice was beginning to lead.

Weeks later, Julian watched one of his earliest videos. The difference was astonishing. His old voice sounded thin and rushed, as if he were trying to keep up with his thoughts. But now, his voice sounded like it belonged to a completely different person—someone confident, grounded, articulate, and deeply present. Someone who didn't just speak to an audience but spoke *with* them. Someone who didn't just share ideas but shaped experiences.

Julian sat back and smiled. He had finally discovered his real voice—not the voice he thought he needed to perform, but the voice that emerged when he aligned his breath, his emotion, his intention, and his presence. His voice had become a tool of influence, connection, and authority. And as he continued growing, he knew one thing for certain: his voice would carry him places his younger self never imagined.

Chapter 8

Mastering Emotional Influence: How to Move Audiences Without Manipulation

Influence is not created by information alone. It is created by emotion—specifically, your ability to shape, guide, and evoke emotional states in your audience. Emotional influence is not manipulation. It is leadership. It is the art of understanding what your audience is feeling, what they need, and how to guide them toward a more empowered, clear, or inspired state. High-authority digital personalities have mastered the ability to create emotional movement in their viewers. They know when to ground their audience, when to energize them, when to challenge them, and when to reassure them. They understand that human beings make decisions emotionally first and logically second. In this chapter, you will learn how to use emotional influence ethically, intentionally, and masterfully to create deeper impact and lasting connection.

The foundation of emotional influence is **emotional attunement**, the ability to sense the emotional state of your viewers even before you speak. Attunement does not require psychic ability—it requires empathy, awareness, and emotional intelligence. When you understand the fears, hopes, frustrations, and desires of your audience, your messages feel personal, relevant, and emotionally resonant. Attunement is often expressed through subtle choices in tone, pacing, facial expression, and story selection. When your audience feels emotionally "seen," they become receptive to your leadership. Emotional attunement is the doorway to influence because people cannot be moved by someone who does not understand them.

Once you establish attunement, the next step is **emotional direction**, guiding your audience from one emotional state to another. This movement is intentional. You may guide viewers from confusion to clarity, from fear to courage, from overwhelm to calm, or from doubt to motivation. Emotional direction begins with acknowledging the current emotional state of your audience. You must let them feel that their starting point is valid. Then, through grounded tone, clear communication, and emotionally aligned language, you guide them toward a more empowered place. Emotional direction transforms your content from passive information into meaningful transformation.

Another key element of emotional influence is **emotional contrast**, the strategic use of shifts in tone, pacing, or intensity to emphasize important points. Emotional contrast creates dynamism in your delivery. When your tone softens before an important truth, viewers feel the weight of your words. When your energy rises slightly during a moment of inspiration, viewers feel uplifted. When your pacing slows before a key sentence, the message lands more deeply. These contrasts keep your audience emotionally engaged. Without contrast, your message becomes flat. With contrast, your message becomes memorable.

The ability to influence emotionally also requires mastering **emotional authenticity**. Audiences can sense when emotion is genuine and when it is performed. Emotional authenticity means aligning your emotion with your message, not exaggerating it. It means allowing your natural emotional truth to be visible without forcing emotion for dramatic effect. Authentic emotion builds trust. Forced emotion destroys it. High-authority creators show emotion with restraint, subtlety, and intention. They avoid extremes that feel theatrical. They focus on truthful emotional expression that strengthens connection rather than seeking sympathy or attention.

Another crucial part of emotional influence is **the power of specificity**. Vague emotional language does not create emotional movement. Specific emotional language does. Statements like “This can be stressful” are less powerful than “It feels like your mind is spinning so fast you can’t even breathe.” Specific emotions trigger deeper resonance because viewers feel understood. The more precisely you can describe emotional experiences, the more impact your content has. Specific emotional language also positions you as a creator who understands people at a deeper level, increasing your authority.

Storytelling is another essential tool of emotional influence. A well-crafted story bypasses logic and speaks directly to the heart. Stories create emotional immersion. They allow viewers to feel instead of merely think. Emotional influence through storytelling does not require dramatic life events. It requires clarity, relevance, and emotional honesty. When your story illustrates a relatable challenge, insight, or breakthrough, your audience experiences the emotional journey with you. This shared emotional experience builds powerful connection and enhances your influence significantly.

Your emotional influence also grows through **emotional regulation**—your ability to remain centered even when discussing intense topics. Emotional regulation does not mean being emotionless. It means allowing emotion to flow without overwhelming your presence. When you maintain calmness while guiding viewers through difficult emotional terrain, they trust you more. You become a stable emotional reference point. You become someone they can rely on. This steadiness enhances your authority and deepens your connection with viewers. Finally, emotional influence becomes powerful through **consistency and integrity**. You cannot emotionally move an audience if they sense that your intentions are selfish, manipulative, or insincere. Influence built through deceit collapses quickly. Influence built through truth endures. Your emotional influence should always serve your audience. It should never be used to exploit their fears or insecurities. When your emotional leadership comes from integrity, your audience does not feel manipulated—they feel guided, supported, and empowered. This is the highest form of emotional influence: the ability to lead hearts and minds toward growth, clarity, and transformation.

Mastering emotional influence will elevate your digital identity in ways few creators ever experience. It will turn your content into an emotional journey. It will deepen the trust your audience places in you. It will transform your presence into a guiding force that shapes the emotional world of your viewers. When you learn to move emotions ethically and intentionally, you become more than a creator. You become a leader of internal change.

"The Night Julian Learned How to Move a Heart"

Julian had mastered presence, communication, and visual identity, but there was one thing he still didn't understand: why some of his videos felt emotionally flat even when the content was strong. He spoke clearly, confidently, intelligently—but people weren't feeling him. They respected him, but they weren't moved by him. They listened, but they didn't transform. He sensed a missing piece, an emotional dimension that separated technically skilled creators from truly influential ones. The realization came unexpectedly during a live stream where a viewer shared a vulnerable comment about feeling stuck in life. Julian responded with practical advice, but something in the chat shifted. Viewers appreciated his clarity but didn't feel his presence emotionally. Someone finally typed what everyone seemed to be thinking: "I get what you're saying, but I don't feel you with us."

That comment lingered in Julian's mind long after the live ended. He replayed the moment repeatedly, analyzing his tone, his expression, his pacing. He noticed something subtle but important: he had answered the question with logic, not empathy. He had responded with intellect, not presence. He had spoken from his mind, not his heart. And for the first time, Julian understood the truth—he had mastered communication but not emotional influence.

The next day, he recorded a video on motivation. But instead of focusing on structure or delivery, he focused on emotion—his audience's and his own. He imagined what they might be feeling: doubt, frustration, pressure, fear. He acknowledged those feelings out loud before offering guidance.

His tone softened. His pacing slowed. His words became more specific, more grounded, more human. When he rewatched the footage, he felt something new. He didn't just hear himself—he *felt* himself. He sounded present. He sounded connected. He sounded like someone who understood pain and was offering a hand, not a lecture.

The video went live, and the response shocked him. Dozens of viewers said the same thing: "This hit differently," "I felt this in my chest," "I needed to hear it exactly like this." The shift wasn't in his technique—it was in his emotional alignment. He had stopped speaking at his audience and started speaking *with* them.

From that point forward, Julian began studying emotional influence intentionally. He noticed how his favorite creators used subtle pauses during emotional insights, how their voices softened when speaking about pain, how their energy lifted when offering hope. He realized that emotional contrast created emotional depth. He realized that storytelling made viewers feel rather than think. He realized that emotional authenticity created trust more quickly than any perfectly structured sentence ever could.

One evening, Julian filmed a video on dealing with self-doubt. Instead of hiding his own struggles, he shared a moment from earlier in his journey—one where he nearly quit because he wasn't seeing progress. He didn't dramatize it. He didn't exaggerate it. He simply shared it truthfully, explaining how it felt and what shifted inside him. When he spoke, his voice carried emotional texture. His eyes softened. His presence deepened. He didn't perform emotion—he expressed truth. The video became one of his most shared pieces of content. People said they cried, they reflected, they felt understood. One viewer wrote, "You didn't just teach me something—you helped me feel like I'm not alone."

But the moment that changed Julian came during another live Q&A. A viewer asked him how to handle feeling lost in life. This time, Julian didn't jump straight into solution mode. He paused. He breathed. He acknowledged how heavy that feeling can be. He described the sensation in detail—how it feels like drifting through fog without direction, how it feels like wanting to move but being unable to. And then he gently guided the viewer toward clarity. The entire chat slowed down. People thanked him for "holding the moment." They said they felt grounded just listening. When he ended the live, Julian realized that he had finally crossed the threshold between communication and emotional influence.

He didn't feel like a performer. He didn't feel like a teacher. He felt like a leader—someone capable of moving hearts, not just minds. Someone who could guide emotional experience without manipulation. Someone who could create genuine emotional transformation with nothing more than tone, clarity, and presence.

That day, Julian understood the real meaning of influence: not the ability to be heard, but the ability to be *felt*. And from that moment forward, he approached every video with a new intention—to not just deliver information, but to shape emotional experience. He was no longer speaking to an audience. He was leading them.

Chapter 9

Building a Loyal Audience Through Identity, Alignment & Relatability

A high-authority digital personality is not defined by follower count but by audience **loyalty**—the depth of trust, emotional connection, and ongoing alignment between creator and viewer. Loyalty is not earned through constant posting, viral tricks, or high-energy content. It is earned through identity clarity, authenticity, emotional resonance, and the sense that viewers see themselves reflected in you. People do not commit to creators who simply inform them; they commit to creators who represent something—an identity they resonate with, a worldview they trust, and an emotional environment they want to return to. In this chapter, you will learn how to cultivate a deeply loyal audience that stays with you for years, not days.

The foundation of loyalty is **identity alignment**, the sense that your viewers understand who you are and feel that your values, worldview, and emotional presence match something inside of them. When your identity is clear, viewers know what they are signing up for. They know the tone, the energy, the perspective, and the intentions that shape your message. But when identity is inconsistent—when your personality shifts wildly, your values feel unclear, or your tone varies dramatically—audiences become uncertain. Loyalty cannot grow in uncertainty. A loyal audience is drawn to creators who feel stable, consistent, and aligned with themselves. This does not mean being repetitive or rigid; it means being reliably *you*.

Next, loyalty emerges through **relatability**, the bridge that connects your internal world to your audience's internal world. Relatability is not achieved by oversharing or performing vulnerability. Instead, it arises from expressing your experiences, emotions, and challenges with honesty, humility, and clarity. When viewers hear pieces of their own story within your story, they feel connected. When they see their fears reflected in your words, they feel understood. When they recognize their hopes in your guidance, they feel inspired. Relatability is not about being like everyone else; it is about allowing your audience to see themselves in your evolution, your lessons, your decisions, and your human moments.

Another pillar of audience loyalty is **message consistency**, the repetition of core themes that reinforce your identity. Your audience should be able to articulate what you stand for without hesitation. Consistent messaging builds trust and memorability. When your themes are scattered or inconsistent, your viewers cannot form an emotional anchor. But when your values and messages repeat across videos, stories, and formats, your presence solidifies in their minds. Your audience begins quoting you, referencing your ideas, and relying on your frameworks. Consistency is the glue that turns viewers into followers and followers into loyal supporters.

Loyalty also grows through **emotional safety**, the sense that your presence provides stability, clarity, and reassurance. When viewers feel emotionally safe in your content, they return again and again. They trust your tone, your temperance, and your perspective. They know you will not belittle them, confuse them, overwhelm them, or destabilize them. High-authority creators create emotional environments that feel stable and grounded. They speak with emotional clarity. They maintain composure. They express empathy without indulging in emotional chaos. When viewers feel emotionally safe with you, their loyalty deepens.

A loyal audience is also nurtured through **reciprocal value**, the sense that you genuinely care about their growth, clarity, and transformation—not just their engagement. This value can manifest through thoughtful insights, emotionally supportive commentary, or practical guidance that helps viewers grow. When viewers feel that your content improves their lives in meaningful ways, they form an emotional bond with you. Loyalty does not form around creators who seek attention; it forms around those who provide value that feels real, relevant, and consistent.

A powerful but often overlooked component of loyalty is **narrative continuity**. People stay connected to creators whose stories they can follow. When your audience witnesses your growth, challenges, milestones, and evolution, they feel invested. Narrative continuity does not require dramatic announcements or constant life updates. It simply means showing up with honesty, sharing relevant insights from your personal journey, and allowing your audience to observe the evolution of your identity over time. Humans are wired for story. When your story feels alive and authentic, your audience becomes part of it.

Another factor in loyalty is **recognizable emotional energy**. Your viewers should know how they will feel after consuming your content. If your presence consistently leaves them grounded, inspired, empowered, or soothed, they will keep returning. The emotional outcome is part of your brand. Your energy becomes part of their emotional routine. This is why emotional consistency is essential. When your energy fluctuates unpredictably, the emotional experience becomes unreliable. But when your energy is steady, viewers naturally gravitate toward the emotional comfort you provide.

Finally, audience loyalty becomes powerful through **long-term integrity**. Your audience forms loyalty not just from what you say, but from what you *do* over months and years. When your actions match your message, your authority strengthens. When you maintain honesty, transparency, and grounded leadership—even when facing challenges or criticism—your audience sees your character. Integrity is the ultimate binding agent of loyalty. It is what transforms followers into communities and communities into movements.

Building a loyal audience is not about trends, virality, or entertainment gimmicks. It is about creating emotional resonance, identity clarity, and a stable presence that viewers can trust. When you build loyalty through alignment, relatability, consistency, emotional safety, narrative continuity, and integrity, your audience doesn't just watch your content—they grow with you. And once you achieve that, you are no longer simply a creator. You become a trusted guide in the inner lives of thousands.

"The Moment Julian Realized Loyalty Isn't Won—It's Earned"

Julian had built a strong following by now. His presence was grounded, his communication sharp, his visuals polished, and his voice resonant. But something still nagged at him: although he had thousands of followers, only a small portion felt truly connected. Most viewers watched a few videos and left. He had an audience, but he didn't yet have a *loyal* audience. One night, after posting a deeply personal video about his early struggles with doubt, he noticed something unusual in the comments. The same names kept appearing—people who had followed him for months, who remembered details he had shared, who celebrated his progress. They weren't casual viewers. They were something else. They felt connected to him. That was when Julian realized loyalty wasn't about numbers. It was about relationship.

He rewatched several of his older videos trying to figure out why strangers felt connected to some videos more than others. He noticed a pattern quickly. In the videos where he allowed himself to be grounded, human, and emotionally present, viewers responded with warmth and resonance. In the videos where he focused solely on information or performance, viewers responded politely but not deeply. It dawned on him that loyalty came from alignment—between who he was and what he expressed. When he hid his real experiences, he felt distant. When he shared them thoughtfully, he felt relatable.

A turning point came during a Q&A livestream. A viewer asked him if he had ever felt like an imposter. For the first time, Julian didn't give the polished, distant answer he used to rely on. He took a breath. He acknowledged the fear honestly. He talked about nights when he doubted everything, when he questioned whether anyone cared, when he wondered if his content even mattered. He didn't dramatize it. He didn't make it a spectacle. He simply told the truth. The chat exploded with connection. People shared their own fears. They thanked him. They said they felt less alone. And in that moment, Julian realized that leadership wasn't about perfection—it was about connection.

Over the next several weeks, Julian experimented with being clearer about his identity and values. He didn't change who he was—he simply became more consistent. He spoke from the same emotional center in every video. He reinforced the same core messages of growth, clarity, groundedness, and self-belief. He wasn't trying to be everything to everyone. He was allowing himself to be something specific for the people who resonated with him. And something incredible happened: those people stayed. They engaged more. They shared his content. They treated his videos as part of their routine, as if his voice and presence had become a meaningful part of their day.

But the most profound moment occurred when Julian shared a story he had avoided for years—a moment from his early journey when he nearly quit because he felt invisible. He didn't share it to be dramatic. He shared it because he knew someone out there felt the same. In the comments, a viewer wrote, "This is why I follow you. You talk about the things most creators avoid. You tell the truth without judgment." Others echoed the sentiment. They mentioned how grounded and safe he made them feel, how consistent his presence had become, how they trusted him because he never tried to be someone he wasn't. Julian realized that loyalty was forming not because he crafted a persona, but because he allowed his real identity—refined, grounded, intentional—to be visible.

Another moment of growth came during a collaboration. The other creator constantly shifted tone, style, and personality depending on the topic. His audience seemed confused, half-engaged, unsure of who he really was. Julian observed this and saw a reflection of who he used to be—scattered, adaptive, disconnected from himself. When Julian spoke, his tone remained steady. His presence remained grounded. His values remained clear. He didn't shift to impress. He didn't alter his identity to fit the moment. And afterward, people commented on how "Julian felt like the same person no matter the topic." That was when he understood the power of identity alignment.

As months passed, Julian watched quietly as something beautiful unfolded. His comment section filled with familiar names. People referenced things he said months earlier. They told him they felt like they knew him. They thanked him for his consistency. They said his presence made them feel at home. He had become someone they trusted—not because he shouted the loudest, but because he showed up the truest. He provided emotional safety. He provided clarity. He provided continuity. Julian realized that loyalty wasn't something you won—it was something you earned through truth, consistency, and emotional presence. His audience didn't stay because he was perfect. They stayed because he was aligned. They stayed because he was real in a refined, grounded, intentional way. They stayed because they saw themselves in his journey. And for the first time in his creator life, Julian felt the weight and privilege of what he was building—not a following, but a community.

Chapter 10

Becoming an Unforgettable Digital Personality: Your Signature Identity in Action

Becoming a high-authority digital personality is not the result of a single skill, but the integration of every skill you've developed—your presence, voice, emotional intelligence, communication framework, visual identity, confidence, clarity, and grounded leadership. When these elements merge into a single coherent expression, something profound happens: you become unforgettable. Your personality stops being something you perform and becomes something you *embody*. You move beyond mechanics and technique into the realm of identity—an identity so aligned, consistent, and emotionally resonant that your audience recognizes you instantly. In this final chapter, you will learn how to fuse all previous chapters into a cohesive signature identity that elevates you from "a creator" to "a personality."

The foundation of an unforgettable digital personality is **identity integration**, the seamless alignment between your inner world and your outward expression. Most creators fail to achieve this because they compartmentalize themselves. They act confident on camera but doubt themselves off camera. They speak with authority but live anxiously. They show one version of themselves in one format and a completely different one in another. This fragmentation creates inconsistencies that weaken authority. Identity integration means that the version of you on camera is not an act—it is your highest, clearest, most aligned self. When your personality is integrated, your audience senses something rare: authenticity without chaos, confidence without ego, vulnerability without weakness, and leadership without pretense. Integration makes you unforgettable because it makes you impossible to imitate.

Another essential element is **signature emotional energy**, the unique emotional atmosphere your audience experiences when they watch you. Every creator who becomes a true digital personality has a signature frequency—a distinct emotional impact that is present in every video. It might be calm wisdom, grounded clarity, inspiring fire, uplifting warmth, quiet strength, or bold intensity. Your emotional signature becomes part of your brand, even if you never label it. This emotional identity becomes your anchor and your magnet. When viewers know exactly how they will feel after consuming your content, your presence becomes part of their emotional routine. That predictability makes you unforgettable. When your emotional energy is stable, aligned, and unmistakably yours, you create a psychological bond that turns casual viewers into devoted followers.

A high-authority digital personality also cultivates **signature thought leadership**, the ability to think, explain, and frame ideas in a way that no one else does. Intellectual originality does not always mean inventing new concepts. It means expressing ideas through your own mental architecture—your metaphors, your frameworks, your phrasing, your perspective. When your audience recognizes your mind within your message, your thoughts become memorable. Your models, stories, and interpretations become mental shortcuts for your viewers. They begin quoting you, using your ideas in their own conversations, and viewing their challenges through your frameworks. This intellectual imprint elevates your authority far beyond surface-level content. You no longer give information—you shape worldview.

Consistency is another pillar of unforgettable personality. Not algorithmic consistency, but **identity consistency**. Your viewers should feel the same version of you regardless of platform or format. Your long-form videos, short-form content, live streams, interviews, and collaborations should all reflect the same emotional center, the same voice, the same values, and the same grounded presence. This does not limit your creativity—it strengthens your identity. Consistency becomes a psychological stabilizer for your audience. They trust you because you do not shift unpredictably. You evolve, but you do not fragment. Your transformation is visible yet aligned. This consistency is what anchors long-term loyalty.

To become unforgettable, you must also cultivate **signature storytelling**, the ability to embed meaning into your audience's emotional memory. Stories shape identity. They make your content relatable, human, and emotionally immersive. But unforgettable creators do not simply *tell* stories—they tell stories in a way that reinforces their identity. Their stories reflect their values, their worldview, and their emotional energy. They tell stories that reveal insight without oversharing, vulnerability without chaos, and emotion without performance. Their stories become part of their brand. When your storytelling aligns with your identity, your voice becomes inseparable from the emotional experiences you create.

Unforgettable digital personalities also demonstrate **integrity in action**, the consistency between what they teach and how they live. Audiences may tolerate inconsistency in entertainment creators, but they do not tolerate it in authoritative personalities. If you teach clarity, you must embody clarity. If you teach confidence, you must embody groundedness. If you speak about emotional intelligence, you must demonstrate emotional regulation. Integrity strengthens authority more than any camera skill. When your life and message align, viewers sense a rare reliability. Your presence carries weight because it is rooted in lived truth rather than performance.

Finally, becoming an unforgettable digital personality requires **vision beyond content**. You must understand that your identity is not built from videos—it is built from purpose. Your content simply becomes the pathway through which your purpose expresses itself. When you know what movement you are leading, what transformation you represent, and what emotional or intellectual world you are building for your viewers, your identity becomes larger than the content itself. You become a symbol of a particular type of growth, a particular emotional experience, or a particular worldview. This symbolic identity—rooted in emotional resonance, intellectual clarity, and personal integrity—is what makes you unforgettable.

When you integrate your voice, presence, emotional intelligence, storytelling, visual environment, communication frameworks, and deep internal identity, you become the rare kind of creator who stays with people long after they close the app. You become part of their internal narrative. You become part of their emotional landscape. You become a digital personality who shapes lives, not just videos. This is the level of mastery you have been building toward throughout this book. Now it is time to step into it fully.

"The Day Julian Became Unmistakably Himself"

Julian never knew the exact moment when he stopped feeling like someone trying to grow an audience and started feeling like someone people actually relied on. It didn't happen with a viral video or a sudden spike in subscribers. It happened on a quiet evening when he uploaded a video that felt more *him* than anything he had ever created. The video wasn't flashy. It wasn't dramatic. It wasn't filled with complex techniques. It was simple, grounded, slow, and deeply intentional. And when he watched it back, he felt something he had never felt before: he saw himself—and he saw an identity that had been forming quietly all along.

In those early days, Julian had tried so hard to be confident that he accidentally became performative. He tried so hard to be clear that he became rigid. He tried so hard to be relatable that he overshared. But on this night, none of that was present. He wasn't trying at all. He wasn't performing. He wasn't calculating. He was *being*. His voice felt natural. His posture felt effortless. His gestures were subtle and intuitive. His presence was calm and powerful. His story unfolded without forcing emotion. His insights flowed without strain. He smiled gently at the end of the video, and for the first time, he saw not the version of himself he had trained—but the version of himself he had become.

The comments began pouring in within minutes. Several viewers said, "This is *you*," without knowing how true their words were. Others wrote, "Something feels different in the best way." One viewer left a comment that Julian would never forget: "I don't come to your channel for information anymore. I come for *you*." That was when it hit him. Over the months, something subtle but profound had shifted. People weren't following him for his tips or his frameworks or his polished delivery. They were following him because his identity had become magnetic. He had become a digital personality—not through performance, but through alignment.

From that moment on, everything felt different. Julian no longer worried about how he "should" sound. His voice took on a natural rhythm that didn't try to impress. He no longer rehearsed movements or gestures. His body expressed itself in grounded, understated ways. He no longer panicked about saying the right thing because he trusted his internal clarity. He realized that becoming unforgettable didn't mean becoming louder—it meant becoming truer. The more he embodied his own emotional center, the more his audience recognized something rare in him: a personality that did not waver, did not fragment, did not shift with trends. A personality they could rely on. One evening, Julian filmed a message about resilience. No notes. No script. No preparation. He sat in silence for a moment, then spoke from a place deeper than his mind. He talked about failure, growth, identity, and purpose. His tone was calm, steady, and filled with the quiet confidence he had earned through months of internal evolution. When the video ended, he felt something powerful: he had spoken from his *integrated self.* That was the version of Julian that his audience had been connecting to—the version that was not an echo of other creators, but an original creation shaped by his own experiences, insights, and emotional growth.

During a collaboration months later, the other creator tried to dominate the conversation with high-energy delivery and dramatic gestures. In the past, Julian would have adapted to match the energy. But now, he remained grounded, warm, confident, and slow. While the other creator rose and fell emotionally, Julian stayed steady. Viewers noticed instantly. Comments poured in afterward saying things like, "Julian feels like the anchor," "Your presence stands out even in chaos," and "I trust your energy more every time I see you." This was when Julian fully grasped what he had become. He wasn't trying to stand out. He *couldn't help* but stand out—not because he sought attention, but because he inhabited his identity so completely that he carried an energetic signature no one else could duplicate.

The final confirmation came from a personal message a longtime viewer sent him: "I don't follow you for your content. I follow you because you remind me of the person I want to become." Julian read that sentence over and over, feeling the weight of it. He had become not only a creator but a reference point—an emotional and intellectual symbol for growth, calm, confidence, and clarity.

That night, Julian realized he had finally crossed the threshold. He was no longer playing the role of a digital personality. He *was* one. His identity was no longer shaped by effort—it was shaped by embodiment. He had become the version of himself that he had been building inwardly through every chapter of his journey. And as he closed his laptop, he whispered to himself, "This is who I was meant to be."

Epilogue

Stepping into the role of a high-authority digital personality is not a destination—it is an evolution. By now, you have learned that authority is not a mask, not a performance, and not a set of techniques stitched together for the sake of visibility. It is the result of integrating your voice, presence, emotional intelligence, and identity into a unified expression of who you are at your best. Authority is the natural byproduct of inner alignment. It rises when your internal world becomes consistent enough, stable enough, and intentional enough that your external expression reflects clarity rather than confusion. And when that alignment becomes your default way of being—on camera and off—you transform into a personality that people instinctively recognize, trust, and remember.

The journey outlined in this book is not linear. You will revisit chapters at different stages of your growth. Some lessons will reveal deeper meanings as you mature. Presence will feel different once your emotional intelligence deepens. Your voice will sound different once your confidence stabilizes. Your visual identity will evolve as your internal identity becomes more refined. Emotional influence will shift as you gain lived experience. And your storytelling will transform as your life expands. Each chapter in this book is a practice, not a one-time milestone. You grow into your signature identity the way a tree grows into its shape—slowly, deliberately, and with increasing strength.

If there is one singular truth to take with you, it is this: **the most unforgettable digital personalities are not flawless—they are aligned**. They do not chase trends; they define direction. They do not pretend expertise; they embody wisdom. They do not try to be everything; they commit to being something. Their authority is not loud; it is steady. Their influence is not forced; it is felt. And their presence is not accidental; it is crafted from the inside out through emotional awareness, intentional action, and disciplined self-understanding. When you embrace this truth, you stop trying to "look confident" and start becoming someone who doesn't need to perform confidence at all.

There will be moments ahead when you feel uncertain, when your content doesn't land the way you hoped, when your presence feels shaky, or when the pressure of being visible weighs heavily on your heart. These moments are not signs of failure—they are invitations. Every creator who becomes a true digital personality has moved through cycles of doubt and discovery. Authority is built not only through expression but through reflection. In those uncertain moments, return to your breath. Return to your intention. Return to your identity.

Realign yourself with the emotional core of who you are becoming, and the clarity will return. Presence is a practice. Confidence is a practice. Leadership is a practice. And you are becoming all three.

As you continue your journey, remember that audiences evolve too. They will grow as you grow. They will shift as you shift. They will seek new forms of connection and deeper layers of clarity. Your role is not to chase them, but to guide them with consistency, integrity, and grounded emotional leadership. The viewers who resonate with your identity will stay. They will support you, quote you, trust you, and build a relationship with your presence. You cannot force loyalty—but you can cultivate it by showing up with truth and stability. Over time, your audience will not follow you because of your topics—they will follow you because of your presence. You will become part of their emotional and intellectual landscape. That is the mark of a true digital personality.

This transformation will also expand beyond your camera. As you refine your presence, your relationships will shift. Your conversations will deepen. Your decision-making will become clearer. Your emotional resilience will strengthen. You will bring more intentionality into your daily life, more stability into your reactions, more confidence into your opportunities. The version of you that you have built for the digital world will become the version of you that leads in the real world. This is the hidden gift of becoming a high-authority personality: the work you do on camera changes who you become off camera. The identity you are building is not artificial—it is aspirational. It is your highest expression, practiced consistently until it becomes your lived reality.

And finally, as you move forward, honor the truth that your evolution will never be complete. There is always another layer of presence to discover, another level of clarity to reach, another dimension of emotional intelligence to embody. Your voice will deepen as your life expands. Your presence will mature with every challenge you overcome. Your storytelling will gain richness as your experiences accumulate. You will continue growing into the person your audience already believes you are. This is the beautiful paradox of influence: as you guide others, you grow into your own guidance.

You are leaving this book with more than skills. You are leaving with an identity—a way of showing up in the world that commands trust, inspires loyalty, and reflects the highest version of yourself. You have learned how to breathe with intention, speak with clarity, move with purpose, lead with emotional intelligence, connect with authenticity, and embody your message with grounded authority. This is the foundation of becoming unforgettable. You now carry within you the ability to shape audiences not through performance but through presence, not through perfection but through alignment, and not through pressure but through inner mastery.

Your journey is just beginning. You are ready to step forward as a digital personality whose voice, presence, and identity create real change. You are ready to leave an imprint that no platform can erase. You are ready to become the creator you were always capable of being—confident, grounded, magnetic, trusted, and unmistakably *you*. And as you continue growing, evolving, and creating, remember that the world does not need another loud voice. It needs a steady one. It needs yours.

www.ingramcontent.com/pod-product-compliance
Lightning Source LLC
LaVergne TN
LVHW022007200926
848481LV00007B/2274